THE

PROPHET

HAS

RETURNED

DR. ABRAHAM KHOUREIS, PHD

To Gibran's Enduring Spirit.

And to each one of you…

Table of Contents

Why Has the Prophet Returned?

There are times in history when silence becomes too heavy to carry, when injustice is no longer just a shadow at the edge of society, but a storm sitting at our doorstep.

It is in such times that a voice must rise again, not to create noise, but to call us back to meaning.

This is such a time. So, the Prophet has returned.

He does not come to repeat what was already spoken. He comes to remind us of what we have forgotten. That within each of us is a quiet doer of good, a soul that aches to live rightly, to treat others justly, to lift the world not with grand speeches, but with everyday mercy.

This Prophet is not new, and yet he is needed anew.

He walks in the footprints of the ones before him, particularly, Gibran's Prophet, whose words once washed over our weary hearts like water on stone. They are linked, not by time, but by truth. Not by authorship, but by the same sacred lineage of reform and compassion.

They are of the same prophethood kin, brothers of the spirit, born from the same soil of longing for a more human humanity. Gibran's prophet (ALMustafa, The Chosen One), and my prophet (Raheem, The Compassionate One), breathed the same air, drank from

1

the same water, and rested in the shadow of the same cedar tree. One spoke empathy, and the other compassion.

Though this work stands apart from Gibran's original masterpiece, its concept was inspired by its enduring spirit. A century ago, Gibran gave the world a voice that awakened hearts to listen more deeply. Today, my prophet speaks to a different time and a different world, yet carries the same calling, to remind us of who we are.

My Prophet speaks now because the world is bleeding now. Because kindness has been mistaken for weakness. Because power is loud, but justice remains hushed.

Prophet Raheem comes to stand for those whose voices have been drowned, whose presence has been overlooked, whose dignity has been deferred.

His return is not about prophecy. It is about responsibility. It is about accountability. To wake the sleepers. To comfort the aching. To stir the doers of good who have grown silent. To remind us that we belong to one another, not by law, but by our shared humanity.

If Gibran's Prophet taught us how to feel (Empathy), this prophet comes to teach us how to act (Compassion).

Raheem is no savior. No saint. But he is our inner reminder we can no longer ignore, calling us back to ourselves, and forward into the world we still have time to make better.

How It All Began

He arrived not by plane, nor bus, nor train. He crossed no border. No passport stamped him in. No camera captured his crossing. He simply appeared, as if time remembered him and space made room for his arrival.

On the edge of Los Angeles, just as the sky was peeling back its night, he stood beneath a bent streetlamp that flickered like a pulse and waited.

The streets were wet from a light rain, not enough to clean the city, but just enough to soften it. Neon signs still buzzed from hours that never sleep. Billboards loomed overhead with promises too large to keep.

A USPS delivery truck passed. Then a woman walking her dog. Neither saw him, but both slowed down, as if something had shifted, some presence had entered that the skin could feel even if the eye could not see.

He wore no crown, no mark of divinity. Just an old soft robe, well-walked shoes, and the kind of face that makes you wonder if you have met him before in a dream or a memory.

Prophet Raheem stepped onto Hollywood Boulevard like a man returning to a place he had once prayed for. Not with fame, but with love.

He looked up at the downtown skyline, glittering with glass, humming with ambition. He saw towers built from dreams and sidewalks paved with forgotten names.

He whispered, so quietly even the wind had to lean in:

I am Prophet Raheem (The Compassionate One),

I have returned not to be seen,
but to make you see again.

The city was still half-asleep, but something ancient had awakened. A voice that had not spoken in ages, 102 years to be exact, now stood among them again, not in memories, but in the flesh of a man who had walked through silence to speak once more.

On Hope

The first scene Prophet Raheem witnessed was of an elderly lady with wrinkled tired hands. She looked up and saw his gentle spirit. And without hesitation, she asked him, "Master, I am tired, is their hope?"

He knelt beside her and said:

Hope is not a promise. It does not come wrapped in certainty, nor does it guarantee you shall win or rise.

Hope simply says, if you are tired, try again,
even when your knees bleed and your voice breaks.

Some will tell you hope is naive.

But I tell you, hope is the most defiant form of wisdom.

It knows the weight of history yet still believes in a tomorrow not yet written.

Hope is different from wishing.

Wishing waits.

Hope moves.

It is the trembling step forward in the dark when your heart tells you there might still be a dawn.

You will not find hope in speeches,
nor always in scripture.

You will find it in the man who opens his shop after war has burned the street.

In the woman who plants seeds in soil soaked with grief.

In the prisoner who hums a song only he remembers.

Hope is a silent rebellion against despair.

It does not shout. It does not march.

It stays.

It moves forward.

Staying and moving forward is sometimes the greatest act of courage.

Do not expect hope to remove your pain.

It is not an escape; it is a companion.

It sits with you in the ache, and it reminds you, you are not finished yet.

It is a gentle reminder that you will overcome.

So, if you carry hope today, do not wear it like a medal.

Wear it like a torch, for someone else who cannot yet see their way.

Light their path and walk slowly.

Although you are tired, slow down, catch up, and when you and they are ready, move forward together.

On Grief

The second scene he witnessed was a funeral of an Angeleno child who had passed away from a drive by shooting. Prophet Raheem stood beneath an old oak tree where the people gathered in silence, their eyes heavy with loss.

One of them approach him and asked, "Please speak to us of grief."

Prophet Raheem (The Compassionate One) said:

Grief is the ache of love with no place to go.

It is not the absence of joy, but its echo in a hollow room.

It knocks on your chest like a child at a locked door, not to punish you, but to remind you that something precious was once inside.

Do not hush your sorrow.

Let it cry.

Let it collapse into your lap with all its weight and weep through your body.

That is how it leaves in parts, through the sigh, the shiver, the silence that follows.

Grief is not your enemy. It is a tailor, sewing your soul back together with invisible thread. Each stitch a memory. Each knot a lesson. Each tear a sacred act of remembering.

The world has taught you to be ashamed of your tears, but I say to you:

Let them fall.

Let them fall like rain over dry land.

If you ask me how long grief stays.

I tell you this, grief never truly leaves.

It changes clothes.

It may walk quieter, sit softer, and laugh sometimes.

But it remains a loyal shadow to the love that shaped you.

Do not chase it away. Sit beside it.

Say, I remember.

Say, I hurt.

Say, I loved.

That is enough.

Grief is love's way of saying, I still do.

On Justice

An elderly Native-American woman with ash on her hands and a memory of the suffering of her people visible in her narrative eyes stepped forward and asked, "What is justice, and where has it gone?"

Prophet Raheem said:

Justice is not a sword. It is a reflection.

True Justice measures the civility of your society.

Its sword divides.

Its reflection reveals.

One feeds vengeance. The other feeds truth.

You ask for justice as if it were missing.

Justice has never left us.

It is only that many have stopped looking for it where it truly lives, not in the halls of power, but in the quiet cry of the harmed.

Justice speaks in the silence of those buried without names, in the trembling hands of mothers who hold only photographs now.

True justice is born in the unseen.

It rises when a powerful man or woman speaks truth though it costs him or her their place.

When a soldier lowers his weapon because his heart remembers his mother's lullaby.

When a leader kneels not to conquer, but to mourn what his hands have broken.

Justice is not balance; it is restoration.

Not punishment, but remembrance.

Justice is a light that blinds those who have grown too comfortable in shadow.

Dear Ina (mother), if you seek justice, begin with the truth that still terrifies you.

Sit with it.

Let it burn away your pride.

Only then will you be able to say, I have seen myself in the face of the oppressed, and I can no longer be silent.

On Shame

A young, repented hooker with her eyes lowered and her hands folded tightly asked, "Speak to us of shame, for it follows us like a shadow that will not sleep."

And he said:

Shame is not born within you, it is placed there, like a stone inside your chest by hands that never knew how to hold gentleness.

Where guilt speaks of action, shame speaks of identity.

Guilt says, I have done wrong.

Shame says, "I am wrong, even when you are not."

Do not mistake silence for healing.

Shame thrives in silence. It grows in the dark like mold, feeding on secrecy, fear, and the lie that you are alone.

But hear me, and hear me loudly, you are not your shame.

The world will shame you for your body, your voice, your tears, your joy, your resistance, your longing, your race, your religion, your age.

Some will shame you simply because they were once shamed, and they know no other language. You must not carry what is not yours.

Shame, when left unspoken, becomes a mask.

You wear it in the way you shrink, the way you avoid mirrors, the way you say "sorry" when you mean "I exist."

Let the mask fall.

Speak your shame aloud, to someone, to the trees, to the waves, to your own reflection if no one else.

Speak it, and you begin to break its spell.

There is no shame in falling.

There is only shame in believing that falling makes you unworthy of rising.

Do not chase pride to heal shame.

Pride is armor.

And armor is heavy when your lungs need air.

Instead, choose tenderness.

Choose truth.

> Shame cannot stand in the presence of a soul that has made peace with its wounds.

> You were never meant to carry it forever.

> Lay it down. Even if just for today.

> Go live and let live.

On Anxiety

A father with restless fingers and eyes that darted like birds in a storm asked, "what is this thing that tightens my chest though no danger is near?"

He said:

Anxiety is the whisper before the wind. The ache of what might come, even if it never does. It is the mind rehearsing harm that hasn't happened, and the heart bracing for a wound it cannot name.

It is born where control is lost, fed by uncertainty, and sheltered in silence. The body may be still, but inside, everything races, thoughts collide, breaths shorten, and peace feels like a far-off shore.

Do not mock your anxiety. It is a signal, not a sentence. It means you are deeply alive, sensitive to the world's tremors, attuned to things others dismiss.

But know this:
Anxiety is a voice, not the truth. It warns, but it does not decide. You may walk with it, but do not let it walk for you.

Speak gently to your fear, as you would to a frightened child. Say, "I see you, but I must keep going."

Anxiety thrives in isolation. It shrinks in shared spaces, a listening ear, a hand held without explanation, a breath taken slowly, together.

You are not weak for feeling overwhelmed. You are human. And healing is not the absence of anxiety, but the courage to keep living alongside it, without letting it close your eyes to the light.

On Stress

A merchant with sore shoulders and a soul stretched thin asked, "what is stress, and why does it follow me even when the task is done?"

He said:

Stress is not just the weight of doing. It is the cost of carrying too much for too long without rest, without recognition, without release.

It begins quietly, with small compromises.
A skipped breath. A missed sunrise.
A smile forced when your spirit is tired.

Stress grows when you become what others need but forget what you yourself need. It is the tension between who you are and what you are asked to endure.

The world may call it ambition or responsibility. But stress, when left unnamed, becomes a thief. It steals sleep, softens joy, and turns kindness into irritability.

You do not need to earn your rest. You are not a machine. Even the earth rotates into night. Even the oceans pause. Do not be ashamed to stop. Stillness is not laziness. It is wisdom.

It is the body's way of saying,

"I have done enough. Let me be held."

Learn to listen before your body must shout. Before the headache speaks, before the breath shortens, before your patience crumbles.

You are not failing when you rest. You are preserving what is sacred. You are worthy, not for how much you carry, but for the courage to put things down.

On Depression

A young man who smiled without meaning and laughed without joy asked, "What is this heaviness I carry, though nothing seems to be wrong?"

Prophet Raheem said:

Depression is not always born of tragedy. Sometimes it comes like a fog, without cause, without warning, silent, quiet, and uninvited, wrapping itself around the soul.

It is the silence between loud thoughts, the emptiness in a room full of people. It is waking with breath but not with will.

Do not call the depressed lazy, for you do not see the battle behind their stillness. Even rising from bed can feel like lifting the world.

Depression is not sadness. Sadness moves like a wave. Depression settles, like dust that refuses to lift. It does not scream. It dims. It is a light turned low, a song that no longer stirs the heart.

If you feel this weight, know that you are not broken. You are not alone. You are not weak for not being able to smile through it.

Seek help. There is no shame in needing help. The strongest cry not when they are shattered, but when they trust someone enough to witness the breaking.

Let others in, even if only a crack. Let their light leak through your darkness, until slowly, day by day, your own begins to return.

Healing does not always look like joy. Sometimes it is simply showing up, eating one bite, standing in the sun, or remembering that tomorrow still exists.

You are not your pain. You are the one carrying it.

Even now, you are still here. And that is no small miracle.

.

On Homelessness

An old woman with weathered skin and eyes like unanswered prayers asked, "What does it mean to have no home, and why do they not see me?"

And he said:

Homelessness is not just the absence of shelter. It is the absence of belonging. It is being seen and still invisible. It is asking for help with dignity and receiving silence in return.

To be homeless or unhoused is to carry your life in bags, your memories scattered, your safety conditional, your worth questioned by strangers who pass with pity or scorn.

But know this.

Home is not only walls and doors. It is a place where your name is safe. Where you can sit without being moved along. Where you are not measured by what you own, but by the simple truth that you exist.

Many speak of the poor, but few sit beside them. Many give to the hungry, but fewer ask their names.

Some lose homes through misfortune. Some through war. Some through the failure of societal and financial systems built to serve only the few. And some are born into a world that never had a place for them.

No one chooses to be forgotten. No one dreams of sleeping beneath judgment.

If you want to understand homelessness, look not at the man beneath the bridge, but at the society that built no path back for him.

If you have a home, let it never harden your heart.

Let it make you kinder, more willing to share the warmth that others are denied. Because the measure of a people is not in how high their towers rise, but in how low they are willing to kneel to lift another from the cold.

On Mindfulness

A young Japanese woman touring Los Angeles, spilled water yet watched it ripple with wonder asked, "What is mindfulness, and why does the moment run from me so quickly?"

He said:

Mindfulness is the art of being where your feet are, not just where your plans or worries have gone. It is the noticing of now, the quiet witness to a breath, a glance, a falling leaf.

The world will rush you. It will pull your mind toward the undone and the uncertain. But mindfulness whispers,

"Be here. All of you. Just here."

It is not an escape from reality.

It is a return to it.
Not to fix the past, nor to control the future, but to fully touch the life you are already living.

When you eat, taste. When you speak, mean it.
When you walk, know the ground that carries you.

You do not need a mountaintop to be mindful. You only need to pause long enough to feel the moment without trying to hold it.

Mindfulness is not stillness without thought. It is awareness with tenderness. To feel an emotion without drowning in it, to witness a pain without naming it your forever.

The mindful ones are not detached. They are deeply present. They love more honestly, for they are not elsewhere when you speak.

When you live this way, you begin to see the sacred in small things, the way sunlight touches a window, the sound of your own breath forgiving you, the way now never repeats itself.

Mindfulness is not an achievement.

It is an invitation, to live before life passes through your fingers unnoticed.

On Truthfulness

A Christian priest with a Holy Bible in his hands and inquisitive questions in his heart asked, "Tell us about truthfulness. Is it always good to speak the truth?"

He said:

Truthfulness is not the sharing of every thought; it is the honoring of what is real.

Some believe truth must always be spoken. But I say, truth must first be known and then be carried with care.

Do not mistake cruelty for honesty.

Truth that cuts without healing is not truth.

It is pride in disguise.

Do not mistake silence for lying.

Sometimes truth waits. Sometimes it kneels beside pain until pain is ready to hear.

Never hide behind gentleness to protect a lie.

To lie is to plant seeds of confusion in your own soul.

Each time you twist the truth to be liked, or shrink it to be safe, you teach yourself that you are not enough without disguise.

Speak truth but learn the weight of your words before you let them fall.

The truth told at the wrong time can bruise.

The truth told with the wrong tone can burn.

But the truth told with love, even if it stings, will leave behind freedom.

Begin by being truthful with yourself.

It is easy to lie to others, but the most dangerous lie is the one we feed our reflection each morning.

Ask yourself:

Do I live what I believe?
Do I speak with a tongue that matches

The silence of my conscience?

Truthfulness is not perfection, it is alignment.

It is when your eyes, your voice, your hands, and your soul are all telling the same story.

Be known not for your performance, but for your sincerity.

The world has enough masks. Be the face that breathes beneath them.

On Fear

A woman with calloused feet and a guarded gaze asked, "What of fear? It holds my tongue, stiffens my hands, and wakes me when I try to rest."

He said:

Fear is the shadow of what might never come. It visits before pain arrives. It sits beside your hope and urgently whispers, what if you fall? What if you're wrong? What if they leave?

Hear me loud and clear, fear is not your enemy. It is the trembling servant of your longing to be safe.

It means you still care. It means your soul remembers what loss felt like and would rather shrink than lose again.

Do not curse your fear. Sit with it. Ask it what it is trying to protect. Ask it what wound it remembers. And then tell it gently, you are no longer in charge.

There are those who act without fear. Some call them brave, but often they are just numb. True courage is not the absence of fear. It is the act of walking while fear walks beside you.

You need not conquer fear to live. You only need to stop letting it dictate where you cannot go. Fear will dress itself as logic, humility, even love. But beneath its masks, it is still the voice that says,

Do not risk.

Do not rise.

Stay small.

And you must learn to answer:

I will rise anyway.

When fear comes, name it. Naming turns ghosts into guests.

When fear speaks, breathe.

Breath is the oldest language of your power.

When fear lingers too long, ask yourself, what is the cost of obeying this voice?

You are not made of fear.

You are made of courage, of motion, you feared none when you entered this world, keep fear away, and of rise again, and again.

Fear may visit you and it will, but it must go when it overstays its welcome.

On Peace

A war-torn man with soft eyes and trembling fingers asked, "Where is peace? I have searched for it in silence, in surrender, in solitude, and still, it escapes me."

And he said:

Peace is not found.
Peace is remembered.

It is not a place you go to, but a place you return from, a quiet knowing that you were never broken, only tired from holding the world too tightly.

Peace does not mean the end of pain.
It means pain no longer owns you.

Many chase peace like a prize: in lands untouched by bombs, in homes untouched by hunger, in lives untouched by hardship.

But peace is not the absence of noise, it is the stillness within the noise.

You can sit in a quiet room and feel war within you.

You can sit amid chaos and still carry peace like a heartbeat, no one can silence.

Peace begins when the war within you ends, not by victory, but by embrace.

When you stop fighting your sorrow,
When you stop judging your fear,
When you stop wishing your story was different,
That is where peace waits.

It is not passive.

Peace is the most active surrender.

It is laying down your arms before yourself,
and saying, even here, I am still whole.

Do not wait for the world to be still.

It may never be.

Let peace begin in your next breath.

If you must bring peace to others, bring it not with
answers but with presence.

Do not shout it into their pain.
Sit beside them and become peace.

On Grace

A young mother, weary from giving more than she had, looked up and asked, "What is grace? I give, I forgive, I endure, but I still feel unseen."

And he said:

Grace is the art of giving more than what is deserved, especially to yourself.

It is not pity.

It is not weakness.

Grace is strength wrapped in softness, power disguised as patience.

You were taught to extend grace to others: to forgive, to understand, to offer the benefit of the doubt.

But you were rarely taught to extend it to the one person who needs it most, you.

You are not required to be perfect to be worthy of grace.

You are not asked to finish healing before you speak kindly to yourself.

You are allowed to be both undone and deserving of peace.

Grace is not earned. It is gifted. And when you withhold it, from yourself or from others, you break the cycle that keeps humanity from turning cruel.

To live with grace is to choose tenderness when the world teaches you sharpness.

It is to listen before reacting,
to speak without wounding,
to walk away without leaving harm behind you.

True grace holds boundaries like a mother holds her child, firmly, but with love.

You do not need to understand everything to offer grace.

You only need to see the wound behind the words,
the fear behind the anger,
the longing behind the distance.

And if you ever wonder whether the world notices your grace, remember this:

Grace is not meant to be noticed.
It is meant to transform.

On Faith

A man who had buried too many dreams in the soil of disappointment stood up and asked, "Dear Prophet, what is faith? I believed once. But life broke me."

And he said:

Faith is not certainty.
It is the courage to keep walking when you do not know the way.

It does not live in the answers.
It lives in the asking.
It lives in the pause before the step,
and the step before the path becomes clear.

Some believe faith is a shield; that if you have enough of it, no sorrow will touch you.
But I say, faith is what survives after sorrow touches everything.

Faith is not a bargain.
It is not, If I believe, I will be spared.
It is, even if I am not spared, I will still believe there is meaning in the ruin.

It is not the song of those who have never fallen.
It is the hum in the throat of the fallen who choose to

31

rise again,
not because they are sure they will fly,
but because they remember what it felt like to have
wings.

Faith is not about religion.
It is about remembering that something in you is older
than despair,
stronger than fear,
and more eternal than circumstance.

You do not have to call it God.
You may call it breath.
You may call it light.
You may call it love.

What matters is that you call it back,
especially when you feel most alone.

Faith is not loud.
It does not shout in the storm.
It sits with you in the dark,
places its hand on your back,
and whispers, you are not finished yet.

So let your faith be small if it must.
Let it flicker, let it question, let it cry.
But let it stay.

Because even a trembling faith
can carry you across a crumbling world.

On Courage

A quiet man, eyes filled with old fears and unspoken dreams, stepped forward and said, "What is courage? I have survived, but I have not dared to live."

And The Returned Prophet said:

Courage is not the absence of fear. It is the decision to move while fear still breathes loudly beside you.

It does not always roar. Sometimes it is the softest whisper within you that says, go on, when every part of you longs to stay hidden.

You may think courage belongs only to warriors and martyrs, but I tell you, it belongs to the mother who gets out of bed after another sleepless night,

to the man who speaks his truth after years of silence, to the child who dares to dream in a world that has forgotten how to listen.

Courage is in the refusal to shrink.

In the boldness of showing up again after you have been broken. In the kindness you offer even after betrayal.

Do not wait to feel ready.
Courage does not wait.

It acts, despite the shaking hands, the racing heart, the
uncertain outcome.

Sometimes courage is loud, a leap, a shout, a stand.

But more often, it is quiet, a breath, a "yes," a trembling
step forward that no one sees.

And hear me:

Courage is not only in doing the impossible.
It is also in doing the necessary.

To forgive, when you could hate.
To stay, when running would be easier.
To leave, when staying would destroy you.
To begin again, again.

You were not born to hide beneath the weight of fear.
You were born to walk through it, to speak through it,
to love through it.

Let courage be your companion, not your destination.

And even if you fall, let the world say,
This one fell while rising.

On Privilege

A Caucasian young lady slowly approaches the prophet and attempts to whisper her question afraid the other minority women will hear her. She whispers, "I am not so talented, but so many life and career opportunities come my way because of the color of my skin, tell me about white privilege? "

And he said,

White privilege, and privilege in general regardless of race, is not a crown upon the head, nor coins hidden in the pocket.

It is the unseen road smoothed before your steps, while others walk upon stones that cut their feet.

It is the cup of water placed in your hand while others wander thirsty for a single drop.

It is the voice heard without strain, while another cries until her voice cracks and still no one listens.

Do not despise it, and do not deny it.

For it is not evil to have been given an easier path.

The wrong lies only in forgetting those who struggle beside you, in mistaking fortune for virtue, and in believing that ease is earned while hardship is deserved.

If you awaken to your privilege, let it not weigh you down with guilt, for guilt builds no bridges.

Let it not bind you in shame,
for shame lifts no one from the ground.

Instead, let your awareness give birth to compassion,
and let compassion guide you toward mercy.

For privilege redeemed is not a burden but a gift,
not a curse upon conscience but a blessing multiplied.

Share the smoothness of your road, carry the weary, and spend what was given to you on the good of all.

Create opportunities for others who would not have received them otherwise.

For the true measure of a soul is not in what she receives, but in how she returns it to the world.

On Rebirth

A woman with eyes like old rain and hands that once buried a version of herself asked, "Is there such a thing as rebirth for the living?"

And he said:

Yes.

Rebirth is not for the dead. It is for those who are still breathing and brave enough to begin again.

You do not need to wait for a tragedy to change.
You do not need the permission of endings to start anew.
You are allowed to outgrow your skin, even if it still fits.

Rebirth is not a lightning strike.

It is the quiet moment when you say,

I will no longer betray myself for belonging.
I will no longer stay silent to be safe.
I will no longer carry a name that does not feel like mine.

To be reborn is not to become someone else.
It is to return to who you were before the world taught you to be smaller.

Yes, it is frightening.
To shed the story.
Even if they never knew your truth.

But the moment you say yes to your own unfolding,
the moment you choose the unknown over the
unbearable familiar,
you are reborn.

Not once.
But many times.
You will rise, break, rest, and rise again.
This is not failure.
This is your rhythm.

Some will not understand.
Some will ask why you are no longer who you were.
Smile gently, and say,

Because I finally listened to the part of me that would no
longer wait.

Rebirth is not becoming better.
It is becoming truer.

When you arrive at that quiet place where your name,
your breath, and your soul are in harmony,
you will know:

You have not become new.
You have finally returned.

On Presence

A man who sat beside his family but felt a thousand miles away asked, "Why am I here in body but not in spirit?"

And he said:

Presence is not arriving.
It is remaining.
It is not only being seen,
but truly seeing.

To be present is to give your full self
to the moment you are in,
without rushing past it,
without rewriting it in your mind.

You can be present at a table
or lost in thought a world away.
You can touch someone
and still not be with them.

Presence is not about doing more.
It is about being fully there,
in the conversation,
in the silence,
in the gaze that does not wander.

You are not asked to fix every moment, only to

inhabit it. To hold space for joy without distraction, and for pain without fleeing.

Presence is a gift you offer, and a gift you become.
It is the greatest form of love,
because it says,

"You matter enough for me to stay."

On The Unseen

A woman who swept the floor of grand halls without being thanked asked, "Master, do I matter if no one notices me?"

And he said:

The unseen are not unloved.

They are simply looked through by eyes too busy,
too proud,
or too blind to recognize quiet greatness.

The world applauds the visible,
titles, trophies, voices that echo.
But the unseen keep the world from falling.

They carry burdens others drop.
They show up without invitation,
and give without name.

You may be unnoticed,
but you are not unnecessary.
What you do in silence
becomes the foundation others stand on.

Some lights do not shine from stages.
They flicker in kitchens,
in back rooms,
in forgotten spaces where kindness still breathes.

Do not measure your value
by how loud your name travels.

Measure it by how deeply your presence changes
the space around you.

To be unseen by the world
is not to be unseen by the divine.

Often, the most sacred work
is the kind done in secret.

On Reconciliation

A brother who had turned his back on his siblings asked,
"Can what was once broken ever be whole again?"

And he said:

Reconciliation is not forgetting.
It is remembering without revenge.

It is the moment two souls
step over their wounds
not to erase the past,
but to rebuild something new from its ashes.

To reconcile is not to pretend it never hurt.
It is to say,
"I see what happened,
and I still choose peace over pride."

It does not always end in reunion.
Sometimes reconciliation is silent,
a release,
a letting go,
a soft closing of the door with a bowed head.

But when it does come face to face,
it is a miracle of humility.

It asks each heart,
"Can you make room for what was broken
without needing to win?"

There is no reconciliation
without truth,
without acknowledgment,
without a tenderness that chooses healing
over being right.

Forgiveness may begin in one heart,
but reconciliation takes two.

And when it happens,
even if rare,
it is a holy return.

On The Stranger

A traveler, worn by many roads and welcomed by few hearts, asked, "Why do they fear me when they do not know me?"

And he said:

The stranger is not the one who is far.

The stranger is the one we refuse to see.

People fear what they do not understand,
and they do not know, but more than that, they fear
what they refuse to open their hearts to.

You became a stranger not because you were unfamiliar,
but because they stopped being curious.

They stopped asking.

They stopped listening.

They mistook difference for danger and forgot that every
soul reflects their own longing.

The stranger wears many faces,

the refugee,

the wanderer,

the immigrant,

the newcomer in the country,

the one whose name they do not try to pronounce.

But beneath all those faces is a hunger to be known without suspicion, to be welcomed without question, to be seen without distortion.

The stranger does not need your pity.

They need your welcome.

Your willingness to meet eye to eye,
not as savior and saved, but as human and human.

Do not forget this: You too have been the stranger.

In a new city, a new grief, a new truth you were afraid to share.

When you recognize the stranger in another,
you return to the part of yourself that once longed to be seen.

Let no one remain a stranger because you were too comfortable to cross the distance.

For the stranger you welcome today may become the friend who softens and brightens your tomorrow.

On Belief

A quiet man who stood firm when the wind howled asked, "What is belief, if not something I can prove?"

The Prophet said:

Belief is deeper than faith, quieter than doctrine, and more enduring than praise.

You do not wear belief. You live it.

It is the reason you stand when others sit, speak when others stay silent, hold on when others let go.

Belief is not always loud.

It does not need to be.
Its power is not in how many follow it, but in how fully you embody it, even when no one sees.

What you believe will shape what you choose, and what you choose will shape who you become.

So do not borrow beliefs just to belong.

Let your convictions come from the deepest conversation between your soul and your silence.

True belief asks for courage, not to convert others, but to live with integrity even when your path is lonely.

If your belief makes you kinder and compassionate, you

have heard it well. If it makes you arrogant, you have misunderstood its source.

On Silence

A woman who feared her truth would shatter the peace
asked, "What is the worth of silence when my voice
trembles inside me?"

And he said:

Silence is not absence. It is presence.
It is not always the lack of words,
but the fullness of listening.

There is a silence that hides,
and a silence that reveals.
One buries truth to avoid pain.
The other waits patiently for truth to ripen.

Silence can hold space for healing
or suffocate the heart that longs to speak.
It is not whether you are silent,
but why.

Some speak too soon and scatter wisdom.
Others wait too long and smother it.
But the one who honors silence
knows when stillness is sacred,
and when it is a cage.

There is a silence between two people
that says more than a thousand sentences.

There is a silence before a decision
where the soul gathers itself.

To befriend silence
is to learn the language of your own being.

When you truly listen there,
you will know when to speak,
not to fill space,
but to serve it.

On Deportation

A Mexican woman, her hands trembling from holding too much and belonging too little, asked, "If I did no harm, why am I still sent away?"

And he said:

It is not always crime that is punished.
Sometimes, it is the audacity to seek a better life.

You crossed no lines of the heart,
only borders drawn in ink by hands who forgot their own journey.

You came with dreams,
and were met with suspicion.
You offered labor,
and were answered with handcuffs.

To be called illegal, it is to be told
that your breath is an error,
that your footsteps offend the land they touch

You are not the trespass. You are the reminder
that love, and desperation speak the same language.

They say you must go, but they do not see
the child clinging to your knees,
or the sleepless nights spent building a life
in the shadows of their comfort.

You were never the threat.
You were the reminder,
revealing a system that forgets mercy,
and a people who forgot that their own ancestors
once came with empty hands and hopeful hearts.

What makes a life worthy of staying?
A paper? A number?
Or the simple truth
that no one leaves home
unless the fire behind them burns more than the distance
ahead?

Do not let them name you wrong.
You are not illegal.
You are not invisible.
You are not disposable.

You are a human being with a story,
with sorrow, with sacred belonging.

> Though they may force your body to leave,
> your dignity travels with you.

> Your courage plants seeds.
> And somewhere, someone will remember
> that a stranger once knocked,
> not to take,
> but to be allowed to stay.

On Temptation

A man who stood at a crossroads with both hands trembling asked, "How do I choose peace when my desire calls louder?"

And he said:

Temptation is not the enemy.
It is the reminder.

It shows you where your hunger still speaks,
and what you are willing to risk to feed it.

It is not always the battle between right and wrong.
More often, it is the pull between peace and urgency,
between what heals and what excites.

Temptation wears many faces,
pleasure, escape, validation.
But beneath them all is a question:
"What are you really longing for?"

You will be tempted not because you are weak,
but because you are alive.
You will feel the fire not to burn,
but to learn where your edges are.

There is no shame in being tempted.
The danger is in pretending you are not.

For what you deny in the light
will grow teeth in the dark.

When you face temptation, do not shout at it.
Speak with it.
Ask what it wants.
Ask if it offers peace or only a pause from pain.

Then choose.
Not with shame,
but with awareness.

On Rejection

An elderly mother whose well-off children abandoned her to her old age asked, "Master, tell me, when those to whom I gave my youth, my bread, and my every heartbeat cast me aside in the winter of my old days. Why does being left behind feel like I am not enough?"

And he said,

Rejection is a closed door you still see through. It is the echo that follows you, long after the voice is gone.

To be rejected is not only to be turned away.
It is to question your worth because someone else could not hold it.

But remember:
Their inability to receive you
does not mean you were unworthy.

It means they lost their way.

Rejection feels personal because you gave something personal. And still, it is not a mirror.
It is a moment.

If you live to avoid rejection,
you will shape yourself into what is safe,
and forget what is real.

Not every closed door is a failure.

Some are protection.

Some are redirection.

Some are sacred pauses.

Let your sorrow be honest,
but do not let it rewrite your value.

You are still whole,
even when the dear ones walk away.

On Patience

An elder man who had waited too long and felt forgotten
asked, "How much longer must I endure in silence?"

And he said:

Patience is not passive.
It is the quiet strength to hold steady
when the world rushes past you.

It is the art of standing still
without losing hope.
Of trusting that the unseen roots
are growing beneath your waiting.

The impatient seek relief.
The patient seek truth.

To wait well is to live each moment
as if it matters,
even when the result does not yet show.

Patience is the companion of faith,
the sister of resilience.
She does not shout.
She holds your hand
while time unfolds what you cannot yet see.

Do not rush the story.
Some chapters take longer to bloom
because they carry more weight.

If you are still waiting,
you are still becoming.
And the moment will come
not because you chased it,
but because you were ready.

On Sacrifice

A mother who gave and gave until she disappeared
asked, "Is there worth in losing myself for others?"

And he said:

Sacrifice is not measured by how much you give,
but by how deeply it costs you.

It is not always noble.
Sometimes it wounds quietly,
when no one says thank you,
and no one knows what you laid down.

To sacrifice is to place love above comfort.

To let go of what you hold
so someone else may breathe,
or grow,
or simply make it to the next day.

But let this be clear,
Sacrifice that erases you is not holy.

It is a slow undoing.
Love was never meant to come at the cost of your being.

Give, but not to vanish.

Offer, but not to bleed forever.

True sacrifice is shared.

It leaves room for rest, for return,
for remembrance of who you are.

If you must give,
give from a full heart,
not from a desperate one.

For sacrifice without love is martyrdom.
But sacrifice with love is transformation.

On Regret

An old man whose eyes lingered on the past asked,
"How do I live with what I cannot undo?"

And he said:

Regret is the ache of hindsight.
It is the weight of knowing now
what you could not see then.

It comes not to punish,
but to teach.

To hold a mirror to your former self
and say,
"You were not ready.
But now you are."

Do not run from regret.
Do not let it swallow you.
Let it soften you.
Let it remind you of your capacity to grow.

You are not only your mistakes.
You are who you became because of them.

If you carry regret,
do not use it to chain yourself.
Use it to lift others.

To notice what others ignore.
To choose better when you are given another chance.

Regret does not mean you failed.

It means you care. And that caring can still become something sacred.

On Imagination

A dreamer who drew stars on walls asked,
"Why do they call me foolish for dreaming?"

And he said:

Imagination is not an escape.
It is a compass.
It points not to what is,
but to what could be.

The world was shaped by those
who dared to see beyond what was visible.

Every bridge, every poem, every act of kindness
was once imagined.

Imagination is the soul's rebellion against despair.
It lifts us beyond survival
into meaning.

Those who fear imagination
have forgotten wonder.
They live only in the known
and miss the magic just beyond it.

Imagination does not lie.
It reveals what the heart longs to believe.
And sometimes,
what it dares to create.

Protect your imagination.
Feed it with silence and story.

It will carry you when reason grows tired,
and bring you home to a world not yet built,
but deeply needed.

On Self

A young man, burdened by the noise of who he should be, asked, "Master, who am I when I am no one to anyone?"

And he said:

You are not a single note,
but the music between them.
Not a fixed name,
but the breath that shapes all names.

The Self is not still, young soul.
The Self is a circle in motion.

It rotates gently within you,
carrying your pain,
your pride,
your promise,
each taking their turn,
never staying too long,
never leaving forever.

One day the brave you rises,
next day the broken.
Some mornings you are the storm,
some nights the shelter.

But all of it, yes, all of it,
is still you.

The Self rotates not to confuse you,
but to balance you.

To teach you how to speak
with both your tenderness and your fire,
your silence and your truth.

There is a self that waits in stillness.

It does not shout.

It does not perform.

It watches with compassion.

As the others take the stage,

The self that grieves.
The self that protects.
The self that pretends.
The self that dares.

But underneath them all, there is one,
The one who listens.
The one who heals.
The one who forgives you
before you even ask.

That is the Self within the Self.
That is your home.

That is the inner-you who remembers who you were
before the world told you otherwise.

And when you fall apart,
it is not the end.

It is the rotation beginning again.
It is your wholeness reshaping itself
into ne, a new moment, a new meaning.

So be kind to every version of you.

The loud one.
The lost one.
The one who laughs too late,
and cries too early.

They are all pilgrims,
rotating around a center
called YOU.

"Justice delayed is not justice at all.
It is a wound that remains open,
while the world tells you to heal."

On Justice Delayed

A woman whose cries were met with promises and paperwork asked, "How long must we wait before what is right is done?"

And he said:

Justice delayed is not justice at all.
It is a wound that remains open,
while the world tells you to heal.

It is the promise of fairness,
tied in red tape,
delivered too late
for the ones who needed it most.

Delayed justice teaches the oppressor to wait calmly,
and the oppressed to grow quiet.

It whispers that power matters more than truth,
and timing more than tears.

But truth has no expiration.

Even when buried, it breathes.
Even when silenced, it echoes.

The wait may bend you,
but it does not erase you.

Let your anger be steady.

Let your hope be sharp.

And when justice finally arrives, welcome it, but never forget how long you were asked to survive without it.

On Heaven

An astrophysicist who had searched the skies for answers asked, "Master, where is heaven? Is it above us, beyond us, or is it something we have yet to earn?

And he said:

Heaven is not above.

It is within, and it is here, when you remember how to see.

You were taught to look for paradise in another life, in another place, beyond the clouds.

But I say, heaven is not a destination.

It is a moment when your soul aligns with truth,
when your breath is without shame,
when your eyes recognize another and feel no threat,
only kinship.

The earth is not beneath heaven.

It is not lesser.

It is the womb from which heaven is remembered.

Heaven is not the reward.

It is the reminder of how deeply you have remembered who you are.

71

Do not wait for heaven to come.

Let it awaken in how you love, how you forgive, how you hold even your enemies with care.

Heaven is not tomorrow.

It is possible today, in every word, in every gaze, in every hand extended when it would be easier to withhold.

On Angels and Evil

A priest asked, Master, tell us of Angels and Evil.

And he said:

They are forces, born from your own depths.
Angels rise each time you choose compassion when
cruelty feels easier. Evil stirs each time you betray your
own knowing for the taste of power, revenge, or pride.

The angel is not a winged creature. It is the moment you
pause to see another as yourself. It is the whisper that
says, wait, listen, forgive. It is the softness that remains
even after the world hardens you.

And Evil,

Evil is the voice inside that tells you to numb, to
dominate, to forget.

It feeds on your pain and disguises itself as strength.

It says, you are alone. It says, you must take before you
are taken.

But it lies.

You do not need to be perfect to choose the angel
within.

You only need to notice the moment you begin to drift
away from your truth, and return.

Both Angel and Evil speak. Both walk beside your every decision. But neither rules you.

You are the one who chooses which voice to nourish, which silence to honor, which path to walk.

Do not fear Evil.

Fear forgetting that you are still capable of choosing the angel.

You are not at war.

You are the one who ends it every time you choose love and compassion.

On God

A doubtful philosopher who keeps seeking and worn by silence, asked, "Is there a God? And if so, where is this God, when the world burns and I can no longer feel them?"

And Prophet Raheem answered:

God is not far.

God is not near.

God is not somewhere.

God is everywhere that love remembers itself.

You were taught to imagine God in form, on a throne, in the sky, behind gates or scrolls or books.

But I say to you,

God is not a shape.

God is the space between shapes.

God is not a judge behind a curtain.

God is the breath behind your longing, the stillness that remains after grief has taken everything, the light that does not vanish even when the lamp goes out.

When you cried and no one came, and yet you survived,
that was God, staying with you in the space between
breaking and breathing.

When you offered kindness, you did not have to give,
when you forgave without being asked,
when you wept over the suffering of someone you never
met, that, too, was the presence of God.

God is not always comforting.

Sometimes God arrives as a question you cannot answer.

Sometimes as a silence that refuses to lie. And still, God is
never absent. Only misnamed.

You ask where God is in war,

in hunger,

in cruelty.

And I ask you, where were you?

There is simple truth, For God moves through you. Not
instead of you.

Do not wait for the skies to part.

Look into the eyes of the broken and still standing.
God is there.

Look into your own reflection when you choose
compassion instead of bitterness.
God is there, too.

You want a voice to thunder.

But God most often whispers,
in the language of trees,
in the preciseness of the universe's movement,
in the silence between your thoughts,
in the moment you realize you are still here,
and somehow, still soft.

You will not find God in answers.
You will find God in your honest seeking.

Keep seeking, and you will find not a figure,
but a presence that never left you.

You are not separate from God.

You are the spirit and soul of God,
returning home through yourself.

"Self-awareness is not knowing your name but hearing how it resonates in the lives of others."

On Self-Awareness

A university professor who had studied many books but forgotten his own reflection asked, "What does it mean to truly know oneself?"

He said:

Self-awareness is not knowing your name but hearing how it resonates in the lives of others.

It is not the reminder that tells you who you are,
but the moments when no one is watching,
and you still choose to be honest.

To be self-aware is to become a student of your own breath, to ask not only what you do, but why you do it, and who you become each time you act.

Many walk through the world wearing masks,
not to deceive others,
but because they have never looked beneath them.

They confuse their habits with their nature,
and their fears with their identity.

But the one who is self-aware walks gently, not because they doubt themselves,
but because they know how easily harm can hide in certainty.

It is a powerful thing to see yourself clearly, your light and your shadow, your gifts and your wounds, your intentions, and your impacts.

Without self-awareness, wisdom is shallow.
Without self-awareness, kindness is performative.
Without self-awareness, power turns dangerous.

Do not fear what you may find inside. Fear only the life lived blindly, where your footsteps leave harm, you never paused to see.

To know yourself is not a final truth, but a lifelong turning inward.

Those who turn inward with honesty begin to see the world with new open eyes.

To be self-aware is to watch yourself gently, without excuse, without cruelty.

It is the courage to ask,
"Why did I speak that way?"
"Who was I trying to impress?"
"Whom did I hurt when I did not mean to?"
You will not always like what you find,
but that does not make it less you.

It only makes it the part that needs tending, not hiding.

Many decorate their surface,
but neglect the basement of their soul.

They polish their words,
but ignore the rust behind them.

They are known by many, but strangers to themselves.

Self-awareness is not shame.
It is the beginning of wisdom.

It is seeing your own patterns
before blaming the world for their consequences.

The self-aware walk slower,
for they notice where they step.

They speak softer,
for they know the weight of words.

They forgive more freely, for they see in others the same
struggle they meet each day within.

To know yourself is to meet your own eyes not with
judgment, but with responsibility.

In that gaze, if you are honest and unafraid, you will find
not just who you are, but who you are still becoming.

"When you did not yet know yourself,
they called you by your name."

On Caring for Parents

A young lady in her late thirties, encouraged by her husband asked, "Why should we care for our parents when they grow old and weak?"

And he answered:

When you were without strength, they were your shelter.

When you could not walk, they carried you.

When you did not yet know yourself, they called you by your name.

Now their hands tremble and their steps falter.
And you dare to ask, why should we care for them?

Loving and caring for your elderly parents is not a debt to be repaid, but a **circle of life** to be completed.

The tree that once shaded you will one day lean toward your shade.

The well that once quenched you will need water poured back into its stones.

Do not call it burden, for in truth it is blessing.

For what greater gift than to return tenderness and kindness to those who first gave it without measure.

Remember: as you care for them, so shall your children learn to care for you. The measure you give will be the measure you receive.

Honor your parents in their older fading days,
for one day you will be honoring yourself.

On Detaining Migrants

An Ice Agent with a compassionate heart moved by the scene of how people surrounded the prophet, took his turn, and asked, "What is my duty toward those imprisoned behind these walls? They are illegals. Am I to be blamed for them being detained, deported and leaving loved ones behind?"

And he said,

"You see them as illegal, yet they were human before they crossed,
and they remain human after.

Do not mistake their lack of legal papers for the absence of a soul.

If you treat them only as cases, you will blind your own heart.

But if you remember their dignity,
even the law in your hand may soften with justice.
Your duty is not only to guard the border,
but to guard the possibility of their belonging to humanity.

The law may detain them,
but do not let your spirit condemn them.

For every migrant who suffers is still a child
of life.

Remember this: when you treat a migrant without
compassion,
you chain your own humanity.

But when you treat even the detained with dignity,
you set both of you free."

On Genocide

A refugee woman whose her entire family had been erased, whose children now lived only in memory, asked, "What is genocide, and why does the world look away?"

He said:

Genocide is not only the taking of lives, but the deliberate silencing of a people's breath, their names, their history, their culture, their belonging.

It begins not with bombs, but with forgetting, when a nation is first made invisible in the hearts of others.

It is not a storm that surprises. It is a plan that proceeds.

With laws dressed in reason, and weapons blessed in prayer. It wears the face of progress while digging unmarked graves.

Genocide does not end with death.

It lingers in the air, in the songs no longer sung, in the land that no longer speaks the language of its people.

And the world?

It turns its face, not because it cannot see, but because it does not want to feel what it knows.

Silence is not neutral.

When you witness injustice and choose comfort, you become a participant and an architect of the cruelty.

But there are those, few, brave, who remember.

And who speak the names the world tries to erase.

Who light candles not only for the dead, but for the dignity that must rise again.

If you have never wept for a stranger's sorrow, you are not yet free.

To stop genocide, one must first believe that another's pain is not beneath their peace.

On Starvation

A Palestinian girl who came to Los Angeles for medical treatment and recovery after surviving the starvation in Gaza, stood before him, her eyes wide with sorrow, her cheeks thin from hunger. Her voice quivered as she asked, "Why are my people being starved?"

The prophet knelt to meet her gaze. He took her hand, fragile like a bird in his palm, and said:

Child, your question is heavy, yet your heart is brave.

Listen closely.

Hunger has walked the earth for centuries.

In distant lands, long before you were born, children like you cried for bread.

Great nations now filled with plenty once endured days when their people searched the ground for maggots and roots.

When mothers gave filthy water in place of milk.

When fathers bowed their heads in shame because they could not feed their own kids.

Those who once were starved have forgotten too quickly.

And now they make others suffer what they once endured. This is the wound of humanity when memory grows faint and compassion fades.

But you, dear child, must also see what endures: goodness.

Look around you, your neighbors are sharing the last loaf of bread, breaking it into small pieces so every hand is filled.

Mothers sing to their children in the night, wrapping them in love when food is scarce.

Fathers lift the weak and carry them, though they themselves are weary. Even in hunger, your people have not abandoned mercy.

Look, beyond your homeland, there are hearts that beat for you.

In places you have never seen,
people gather food, money, and medicine.

They speak your name in prayers though they have never heard your voice.

They write, they march, they send what little they have.

For compassion is not bound by walls or borders.

Take courage, little one. Your people are not forgotten.

Starvation may weaken the body, but it cannot touch the strength of your people who choose to love one another during hunger. Nor can it silence the goodness of strangers across the earth who call you their own.

Remember: even in hunger, humanity lives. If humanity and compassion live, hope cannot die.

The Girl's Reply

When the prophet finished speaking, the little one held his hand tighter. Her eyes, though rimmed with tears, glimmered like the first light after night.

She said to him:

"Prophet Raheem, I am only a child, yet I understand. If those who were starved once have forgotten, then I will not forget.

I will remember the songs my mother sang when my stomach ached.

I will remember the bread my neighbor tore in half, so I could eat.

I will remember the strangers across the sea who spoke my name though they have never seen my face.

You say my people are not forsaken, and I believe you.

For if we can share when we have nothing, then how much more will we share when the day of plenty comes?

Prophet Raheem, I may be hungry, but my heart is not empty.

I will grow, and I will tell the world that even in hunger we learned love, even in sorrow we found each other, and even in death we carried life."

Then she released his hand, and though her body was frail, she stood tall as if nourished by hope itself.

On the Cost of Silence

A woman whose patience had worn thin from holding back asked, "What harm is there in silence, if it keeps the peace?"

And he said:

There is a silence that heals,
and a silence that wounds.

The silence that listens is sacred.
But the silence that hides truth,
that avoids pain,
that protects comfort at the cost of justice,
that silence has a price.

Do not confuse quiet with peace.

There are homes where no voices rise,
yet hearts live under siege.

There are countries where the streets are calm,
but the truth lies buried beneath the flags.

To watch suffering and stay silent,
is to join hands with the one who causes it.

There are silences that betray the soul.

When you stay silent to be accepted,
you trade your voice for approval,
and over time, you forget the sound of your own
convictions.

The cost of silence is not always paid in noise,
but in distance.

Distance from your own integrity.
From those who needed your courage.
From the kind of world you claim to wish for.

Some say silence is wisdom.
It can be.

But silence that shelters injustice is cowardice

dressed in calm.

Speak, even if your voice shakes.
Speak, even if your words are not perfect.

Because truth is not always eloquent,
but it is always necessary.

Let your silence be a sanctuary,
not a shield for cruelty.

If you must choose between silence and suffering, choose the voice that trembles, but speaks.

For one voice, raised with love, care, and compassion, can echo louder than a thousand who stayed quiet.

On Ruthless Leadership

A U.S. Marines decorated general with medals on his chest and no rest in his soul asked, "Hey Raheem, is it not strength to rule without mercy?"

And Prophet Raheem said:

Ruthless leadership is not strength.
It is fear wearing the mask of control.

It leads through domination,
not direction.

Through intimidation,
not inspiration.

Such a leader confuses obedience with respect,
and silence with agreement.

They surround themselves with cowards,
not sincere voices.

And in doing so,
they grow powerful in image,
but hollow in truth.

Ruthless leadership builds nothing that lasts.

It forces movement,
but not meaning.

It commands,
but does not connect.

And though it may achieve,
it does so by grinding others down.

Victories built on fear
leave ashes where people once stood.

True leadership does not raise its voice to be heard.
It listens. It lifts.

It walks ahead not to be followed in fear,
but to show a path worth walking.

The ruthless may sit high,
but they are always alone.

Because people may serve out of duty,
but they love only where compassion leads.

A true leader is not feared for their fury,
but trusted for their restraint.

They do not sacrifice people for power,
they sacrifice power to protect people.

Beware of the leader who never weeps.
Beware of the hand that never opens.
Beware of the crown that was taken, not earned.

For the measure of a leader
is not how many follow them,
but how many stand taller because they led.

On Compassionate Leadership

A leadership expert who had been burned by the deceptions of her many leaders asked, "Master, what makes a leader worthy of being followed?"

And Prophet Raheem said:

A compassionate leader does not walk ahead to be admired but walks among them to understand.

They do not rise by stepping on others,
but by raising and uplifting others to their full height.

Leadership is not a crown.
It is a calling.

It is not held by title,
but proven in service.

The compassionate leader does not speak first to be heard. They listen, even when it is uncomfortable.

Even when the truth trembles.

They see people not as tools,
but as souls, each with a history,

a hurt,

a hope.

They lead with firmness,
but not with cruelty.

They make tough decisions,
but never forget the faces affected by them.

To be a compassionate leader
is to stand in power without losing tenderness.

To know that kindness is not weakness,
and humility is not hesitation.

Such a leader is remembered,
not for how loud they spoke,
but for how deeply they saw.

They leave behind more than profit,
they leave behind people who believe in their own worth
again.

A compassionate leader does not demand loyalty.

They earn trust.

And where they walk, others follow,
not because they must,
but because they know they are walking with someone
who would never leave them behind.

The Final Farewell

When all had spoken, when the questions had been
asked, and the hearts had opened like fields after rain,
a stillness filled the space where the prophet sat and
stood.

No one asked this time.
There was no voice, no hand raised, no cry.
Only the sound of being.

Prophet Raheem looked at them all,
the broken and the bold,
the wanderers and the ones still waiting,
and said:

You came seeking answers,
but what you found was your own self,
and your own reminder.

For I have only given you back
what you already carried,

your sorrow,
your longing,
your grace.

You do not need more words now.

You need only to walk with what you have heard.
Not to preach it, but to live it.

Let your love become your voice.
Let your silence carry your strength.

Let your wounds stay open long enough
to let light pass through.

These teachings and reminders were never mine.

They were yours, written in your hunger,
shaped by your joy and pain, and made whole
by your return to what matters most, your humanity.

Remember the heavenly teachings that came before me:

Treat each other as you would like to be treated.

Love one another.

The best among you are the ones who serve others. And
I am adding, "without receiving anything in return."

At this time, they lovingly asked,

"Who are you, Prophet Raheem?" ...

 "Are you heavenly sent?"

He answered, "Let your life be the answer."

"As I am, only you. Just returned to remind you of who
you really are, compassionate decent human beings."

No one spoke after him. Some lowered their eyes. Some
felt tears pressing at the edges of their being, though
they could not explain why.

The Departure

Prophet Raheem walked toward the City of Angels. The streets of Los Angeles, restless and unending, opened before him.

He stepped into them without hesitation. As he appeared before without asking for permission, he disappeared without one either.

A passerby thought they saw him vanish into a crowd of homeless people; another swore a gorgeous and shiny black limousine picked him up as he turned a corner near a row of beautiful buildings.

None could follow his whereabout, none could bid him goodbye. None knew his origin, nor his past, nor if he will return in a hundred years.

Only one thing lingered, "Let your life be the answer." He told them. And you are "compassionate decent human beings."

Recommended Readings

Gibran, K. (1923). The prophet. New York: Alfred A. Knopf.

Khoureis, A. (2025). The Compassionate Leadership Model and Pyramid. Los Angeles: ANG Power Publishing House.

About Dr. Abraham Khoureis, Ph.D.

Dr. Abraham Khoureis, Ph.D., is a multi-talented thought leader and partner, author, an award-winning mentor, and advocate for compassionate leadership. He is an adjunct professor who specializes in teaching graduate-level courses in business and management, blending academic theory with real-world business practices. Dr. Khoureis is also a small business owner and holds numerous state certifications and professional designations and licenses, highlighting his multidisciplinary expertise.

He is the creator of the Compassionate Leadership Model and Pyramid, which emphasizes leadership built on self-awareness, mindfulness, and commitment to serving others without expectation of return. This seven-level model pyramid, with "Community" as its fifth level, reflects his vision of leadership that positively impacts the broader community and society.

Moreover, Dr. Khoureis developed the Disability Learning Attainment Model, a framework designed to empower individuals with disabilities through inclusive education, skill-building, and leadership development. His work champions and empowers inclusivity, accessibility, and ethical practices in both education and leadership. He has been published on *Forbes.com, Newsweek.com,* and the distinguished *Leader to Leader Journal.* He was recognized as LinkedIn's Top

Leadership and Management Voice, and Thinkers360's Top 50 Voices.

Dr. Abraham's contributions extend to his writings, professional development initiatives, and thought leadership, making him a respected emerging leader in the fields of compassionate leadership, organizational behavior, and human resources development.

Readily accessible at:

DrAbeKhoureis.com – DrAbeBooks.com

Social Media: @DrAbeKhoureis

On Amazon.com, search for Dr. Abraham Khoureis

Other Books by Dr. Abraham Khoureis, Ph.D.

The Balance In Between: Finding the Balance Between Emotional Intelligence and Emotional Stupidity.
ISBN: 979-8-989521-12-8

Hollywood Dream: How To Make It In Tinseltown
ISBN: 979-8-989521-17-3

Decoding Microaggressions for Leaders and Beyond: Understanding Microaggressions Face-to-Face.
ISBN: 979-8-989521-14-2

Reasonable Accommodation: Empowering Inclusion.
ISBN: 979-8-989521-13-5

SELF: Introducing The Self Rotating Model.
ISBN: 979-8-989521-15-9

The Compassionate Leadership Model and Pyramid.
ISBN: 979-8-989521-10-4

Revealing The Seven Secrets to Exceptional Mentorship.
ISBN: 979-8-989521-18-0

I am Not Alone. I still Matter.
ISBN: 978-1-966837-23-7

Let Them Go Like a Leader
Powerful HR Insights for Small Business Owners
ISBN: 978-1-966837-17-6

For his latest list of published books, visit:

DrAbeBooks.com – Or visit,

Amazon.com, search for Dr. Abraham Khoureis

THE PROPHET HAS RETURNED

www.ingramcontent.com/pod-product-compliance
Lightning Source LLC
Chambersburg PA
CBHW032049090426
42744CB00004B/140